Four great stories
from the
Old Testament

CONTENTS

Retold from Scripture by Claire Freedman
Illustrated by Arthur Baker

Kevin
Mayhew

A MIRACLE FOR MOSES

Exodus 17:8-16

'Promised Land, here we come!' sang the Children of Israel happily. 'Hurrah! We're no longer slaves in Egypt, but free! Moses, our leader, is taking us to a new country!'

The Israelites thought their troubles were over. They were wrong! Already an army could be seen approaching in the distance. The dreaded Amalekites were coming to attack. 'Do not fear,' Moses told the people. 'Remember, God is on our side.'

That evening, Moses spoke to a man called Joshua. Joshua was brave and trusted in God. 'Pick out the best soldiers from our camp,' Moses told him. 'Tomorrow you will lead the men into battle against the enemy. I shall watch from the hilltop, holding the staff of God in my hand.'

Joshua did as Moses asked. The following morning the Israelite soldiers marched towards the Amalekite army.

Meanwhile, Moses climbed the hill, taking Aaron his brother and Hur, his friend, with him.

'Attack!' Joshua cried. The battle raged fiercely. While Moses held the staff of God up high, the Israelites beat the Amalekites back. But when he lowered the staff, they began to lose!

Soon Moses' arms grew tired. 'I can't hold the staff up any longer!' he cried. Quickly, Aaron and Hur found a stone for Moses to sit on. 'We'll hold your arms up for you,' they told him. With Aaron and Hur's support, Moses' arms never wavered.

By sunset, the Amalekites were beaten! 'Praise God!' the people shouted. And afterwards, Moses built an altar to God in memory of the great victory.

HAILSTONES FROM HEAVEN

Joshua 9-10

At last, the Children of Israel had reached Canaan, the Promised Land. It had taken them forty long years. Old Moses was dead and Joshua was their new leader.

‘God has brought us safely to Canaan,’ Joshua told the people. ‘But we will have to fight for our land.’

Many battles followed. The Amorites and other tribes already lived in Canaan and they had to be driven out. How they hated and feared the Israelites, especially as God was on Joshua's side!

The nearby Gibeonite tribe were also afraid of the Israelites, but they had a cunning plan. 'We'll pretend we come from a far-off country and not Canaan,' they plotted. 'That way we may trick Joshua into signing a peace treaty with us.'

Their plan worked, but when the Amorites found out, they attacked the Gibeonites in revenge. The crafty Gibeonites then asked for Joshua to help them. 'I can't refuse,' Joshua cried angrily. 'Not after signing the treaty!'

The Israelites were outnumbered, but God told Joshua, 'Do not fear. You will win the battle.' Joshua and his men marched all night. They made a surprise attack on the Amorites, chasing them down a steep valley. Then suddenly the sky darkened.

'Look!' pointed Joshua. 'God is sending a terrible storm into the valley!' The Israelites watched in amazement. God was casting down giant hailstones, as big as rocks, onto the Amorite army. Terrified, the Amorites fled in retreat!

‘Thank you, Lord!’ Joshua cried. ‘Hurrah!’ rejoiced the Israelites. ‘God has helped us win the battle!’ And they all praised God for helping them.

THE WATER THAT CAME FROM NOWHERE

2 Kings 3

Israel had many kings, and one was a man called Jehoram. One day, King Jehoram heard some news that angered him. 'The King of Moab has broken a long-standing agreement with Israel,' he told his servants. 'Every year he promises to deliver us 100,000 lambs and 100,000 rams' fleeces. Now he refuses to send anything!'

The servants were alarmed. A broken contract between two kings was serious. This meant war! Jehoram prepared Israel's army for battle. The kings of Judah and Edom also agreed to join the fight.

‘We’ll march to Moab together,’ they said. ‘Through the desert.’ On the journey, their drinking water ran out. ‘We shall die of thirst!’ the soldiers cried.

However Elisha, God’s prophet, lived nearby. ‘Elisha can perform miracles,’ Jehoram’s servants said. ‘He might help us.’

The three kings visited Elisha. He agreed to help and called for a musician. At the sound of music, the power of God fell on him! 'See these dry river beds,' Elisha cried. 'God will fill them with water, without sending rain!'

Early next morning, water came gushing through the land. It flooded the ditches and empty river beds. 'What a wonderful sight!' the soldiers cried, drinking their fill.

Across the desert, the Moabite army saw the water too, but to them the sun's reflection on the water made it look red! 'The rivers are full of blood!' they gasped. 'The three armies must have killed each other; let's get the spoils!' As the Moabites foolishly rushed in, the Israelites attacked, and completely destroyed them!
Another brilliant battle for God's people!

THE MUDDLE IN THE MUD

Judges 4:1-16

God's people settled down happily to live in the new land they called Israel. While Joshua was still alive, they kept God's commands, but after his death, things began to change. 'Let's worship new gods,' the Israelites said. 'We'll build huge statues and bow down to them.'

This angered God, so he allowed Israel to be taken over by their enemies, the Canaanites. The commander of the Canaanite army, Sisera, treated the Israelites harshly. In their misery, the people cried to God for help. God heard their cry, so he told his prophetess, Deborah, to send for a man called Barak.

‘Barak!’ Deborah ordered. ‘God commands you to fight Sisera’s army. Gather 10,000 men and prepare for battle!’ Barak was afraid. ‘Sisera has 900 chariots,’ he cried. ‘We have none. We’re sure to lose!’ But Deborah replied, ‘God will give you the victory!’ Barak was still nervous, but he agreed to go, as long as Deborah came too!

The two armies met at the river Kishon and Sisera's men, in their mighty war chariots, charged towards Barak's soldiers. Suddenly, the heavens opened! Rain poured down! The dry land turned into a muddy swamp!

‘Out chariots!’ Sisera’s men shouted. ‘The wheels are sticking in the mud. Our horses are slipping and sliding everywhere!’ Then the river burst its banks. In the surging flood, Sisera’s chariots were wrecked and swept away!

Now the Israelites attacked! They completely destroyed Sisera's army. Sisera tried to escape on foot but he, too, was killed in the end. 'God has given us the victory!' Barak's men cheered. 'Praise to the true God!'

EVERYDAY BATTLES

Everyone has battles in their life, big and small. It's good to know that with God you don't have to face them alone.

And if you do what is right, God will always be on your side.
Hurrah! Everyone’s a winner with God!

First published in 1998 by
KEVIN MAYHEW LTD
Rattlesden
Bury St Edmunds
Suffolk IP30 0SZ

0 1 2 3 4 5 6 7 8 9

ISBN 1 84003 200 6
Catalogue No 1500224

Front cover designed by Jonathan Stroulger
Illustrated by Arthur Baker
Typesetting by Louise Selfe
Printed and bound in Great Britain